MARK IN A MONTH

The Book of Mark | **30** Days of Reading / Days of Questions

Cover designed by Justin Crabtree http://www.ctreedesign.com

Mark in a Month Copyright © 2012, 2nd ed. Sean McGever smcgever@gmail.com

Thanks

My primary aim in making this booklet was to get the amazing story of Jesus as written by Mark into the hands of my friends. This would be impossible without having access to the Gospel of Mark to share with others. For this I would like to express my incredible gratitude to the team at the NET Bible (bible.org). Their team has produced an easily accessible and highest quality English version for reading and study alike. In particular I'd like to thank David Austin, Executive Director of the NET Bible for his permission to use their translation for this booklet.

I would also like to thank my "Wiffleball Wednesdays" crew from Pinnacle High School who met in my backyard for some Wiffleball and Bible study on Wednesdays for over a year to work through much of this material. I would also like to thank one of my good friends from my days back at Arcadia High School, Rachel Schepenmaker, for her professional editing and helpful comments for this booklet. Rachel and I began following Jesus together at the same time in high school, and she set me up with a cute freshman girl for a school dance that I ended up marrying 7 years later. And of course I would like to thank that cute high school freshman who is now my wife and the mother of our three incredible kids. Thanks, Erin! Last, but certainly not least, I want to thank several men in my life who are lot like Mark, they brought adventure into my life and when I needed it, didn't beat around the bush, but got straight to the point. Thank you Dick, Bruce, Marty, Rick, and Art.

Sean McGever is Area Director for Young Life in Phoenix, Arizona. He also teaches part time at Grand Canyon University, primarily Biblical Interpretation (Hermeneutics), and shares Young Life ideas at ylhelp.com. He is an engineering grad, was a plastic-injection mold nerd, a fiber optic product manager, seminary grad, is still plugging away at degrees without end, but is most known for ordering deep dish pepperoni pizza with extra sauce any time he can.

Introduction

Imagine if you were to go on a month long adventure with a person you've heard lots of stories about, but had never spent any real focused time with in person. I've done this in most of my summers over the last nearly twenty years. People I've known from a distance often have so much more complexity and richness up close and personal, like inching closer and closer to an original true masterpiece at a museum. You wonder the intent and decisions behind each brushstroke.

This little book is a feeble attempt to inch closer and closer to the original true masterpiece of Jesus Christ, the Son of God (Mark 1:2). Many of us have given a glancing look at Jesus. In fact, ideas abound about the importance, relevance, and life of Jesus. Some say Jesus is a wonderful teacher, others a holy man, others a pivotal historical figure...But I want to challenge you to answer a life-changing question posed by Jesus. Jesus asks us, "Who do you say I am?" (Mark 8:29) I am convinced that your answer will be different after inching closer and closer to the account of Mark concerning Jesus, as it has for me.

The Bible provides four accounts of the life of Jesus. I like to tell my high school friends that reading the four gospels is like watching four different news stations report the same story, each with their own different angle. If I was going to call the Gospel of Mark a news station, I might call it "Action News". A lot of my high school guy friends like the Gospel of Mark because it is short (in fact it is the shortest gospel account), and it is all about action. If it were a movie, it would be an action/adventure movie. The opening scene in the first chapter begins with a strange man in the wilderness. The last line leaves the reader in suspense as it describes the disciples being afraid. And what is in the middle does not disappoint. From beginning to end, the Gospel of Mark is a wild ride.

The Gospel of Mark is likely the oldest of the four gospels and is written by Mark, a close friend and associate of the disciple Peter.

This booklet breaks down the 16 chapters of the Gospel of Mark into 30 days of readings and questions. Sometimes the daily reading is only one paragraph, usually it is not much more. The reading is so short that I highly recommend reading the daily reading a few times before moving on to the questions. The questions will require you to look back at specific sections of the reading. Try not to answer the questions from memory, be it from years ago or just moments before. Evaluate each and every word of the Gospel of Mark. Inch closer and closer. I have added my own definitions to terms that may be unfamiliar.

I highly suggest you work through this booklet with a friend or a small group, though it certainly can be done alone. The ideal situation would be to complete the reading and write out your answers to the questions and then meet with others to discuss together.

I hope everyone who works through this booklet gets a lot out of it. But I guarantee that there are some of you out there that will be moved powerfully by the life of Jesus through the words of Mark and you will have 30, 60, or even 100 times more benefit and blessing than you could even imagine (Mark 4:20).

Sean McGever

Day 1 Reading

The Ministry of John the Baptist

1:1 The beginning of the gospel of Jesus Christ, the Son of God. 1:2 As it is written in Isaiah the prophet,
"Look, I am sending my messenger ahead of you,
who will prepare your way,
1:3 the voice of one shouting in the wilderness,
'Prepare the way for the Lord,
make his paths straight.'"
1:4 In the wilderness John the baptizer began preaching a baptism of repentance for the forgiveness of sins. 1:5 People from the whole Judean countryside and all of Jerusalem were going out to him, and he was baptizing them in the Jordan River as they confessed their sins. 1:6 John wore a garment made of camel's hair with a leather belt around his waist, and he ate locusts and wild honey. 1:7 He proclaimed, "One more powerful than I am is coming after me; I am not worthy to bend down and untie the strap of his sandals. 1:8 I baptize you with water, but he will baptize you with the Holy Spirit."

The Baptism and Temptation of Jesus

1:9 Now in those days Jesus came from Nazareth in Galilee and was baptized by John in the Jordan River. 1:10 And just as Jesus was coming up out of the water, he saw the heavens splitting apart and the Spirit descending on him like a dove. 1:11 And a voice came from heaven: "You are my one dear Son; in you I take great delight." 1:12 The Spirit immediately drove him into the wilderness. 1:13 He was in the wilderness forty days, enduring temptations from Satan. He was with wild animals, and angels were ministering to his needs.

Preaching in Galilee and the Call of the Disciples

1:14 Now after John was imprisoned, Jesus went into Galilee and proclaimed the gospel of God. 1:15 He said, "The time is fulfilled and the kingdom of God is near. Repent and believe the gospel!" 1:16 As he went along the Sea of Galilee, he saw Simon and Andrew, Simon's brother, casting a net into the sea (for they were fishermen). 1:17 Jesus said to them, "Follow me, and I will turn you into fishers of people." 1:18 They left their nets immediately and followed him. 1:19 Going on a little farther, he saw James, the son of Zebedee, and John his brother in their boat mending nets. 1:20 Immediately he called them, and they left their father Zebedee in the boat with the hired men and followed him.

Isaiah (1:1) A prophet from the Old Testament around 700 B.C.
Repentance (1:4) A change of mind that will be acted on in the future
Spirit (1:10) The Holy Spirit, God, a member of the Trinity
Gospel (1:15) The good news about God and His relation to people

Day 1 Questions

We all could use a new beginning. Maybe today is a good starting place for your life.

1. What does the first sentence in the book of Mark tell us about its purpose? (1:1-8)

They are preparing the way for the Lord

2. Jesus endured temptations from Satan. How do you think He had the strength to do this? (1:9-1:13) *He had God with him. He was sent by the Lord, so he knew he was safe*

3. What do you think it means to "repent and believe in the gospel"? (1:14-1:20)

Confess your sins, and ask for forgiveness

Take a moment to reread this section.

1. What is one question you have from Day 1?

Why was Jesus sent into the wilderness

2. What is one phrase or idea that catches your attention or speaks to you from Day 1?

1:8 "I baptize you with water, but he will baptize you with the Holy Spirit

3. In a word or a short phrase, what is one thing you learned about Jesus from Day 1?

He is powerful

4. Based on what has happened in your life in the last 24 hours, why do you think God had you read this today?

I want a new beginning in my faith

Day 2 Readings

Jesus' Authority

1:21 Then they went to Capernaum. When the Sabbath came, Jesus went into the synagogue and began to teach. 1:22 The people there were amazed by his teaching, because he taught them like one who had authority, not like the experts in the law. 1:23 Just then there was a man in their synagogue with an unclean spirit, and he cried out, 1:24 "Leave us alone, Jesus the Nazarene! Have you come to destroy us? I know who you are – the Holy One of God!" 1:25 But Jesus rebuked him: "Silence! Come out of him!" 1:26 After throwing him into convulsions, the unclean spirit cried out with a loud voice and came out of him. 1:27 They were all amazed so that they asked each other, "What is this? A new teaching with authority! He even commands the unclean spirits and they obey him." 1:28 So the news about him spread quickly throughout all the region around Galilee.

Healings at Simon's House

1:29 Now as soon as they left the synagogue, they entered Simon and Andrew's house, with James and John. 1:30 Simon's mother-in-law was lying down, sick with a fever, so they spoke to Jesus at once about her. 1:31 He came and raised her up by gently taking her hand. Then the fever left her and she began to serve them. 1:32 When it was evening, after sunset, they brought to him all who were sick and demon-possessed. 1:33 The whole town gathered by the door. 1:34 So he healed many who were sick with various diseases and drove out many demons. But he would not permit the demons to speak, because they knew him.

Praying and Preaching

1:35 Then Jesus got up early in the morning when it was still very dark, departed, and went out to a deserted place, and there he spent time in prayer. 1:36 Simon and his companions searched for him. 1:37 When they found him, they said, "Everyone is looking for you." 1:38 He replied, "Let us go elsewhere, into the surrounding villages, so that I can preach there too. For that is what I came out here to do." 1:39 So he went into all of Galilee preaching in their synagogues and casting out demons.

Cleansing a Leper

1:40 Now a leper came to him and fell to his knees, asking for help. "If you are willing, you can make me clean," he said. 1:41 Moved with compassion, Jesus stretched out his hand and touched him, saying, "I am willing. Be clean!" 1:42 The leprosy left him at once, and he was clean. 1:43 Immediately Jesus sent the man away with a very strong warning. 1:44 He told him, "See that you do not say anything to anyone, but go, show yourself to a priest, and bring the offering that Moses commanded for your cleansing, as a testimony to them." 1:45 But as the man went out he began to announce it publicly and spread the story widely, so that Jesus was no longer able to enter any town openly but stayed outside in remote places. Still they kept coming to him from everywhere.

Sabbath (1:21) Saturday, the Jewish formal day of rest
Synagogue (1:21) A Jewish meeting place, similar to a modern church
Leper (1:40) A person with a skin disease which brought numbness and significant skin damage
Moses (1:44) Jewish leader who led Israel out of Egypt, received the law and Ten Commandments

Day 2 Questions

Jesus was always teaching and healing people. What do you need to learn to-day? Where do you need God's healing touch today?

1. What does the unclean and evil spirit teach us about Jesus? (1:21-1:28)

2. When this lady was healed, what was her response? Why do you think she did this? (1:29-1:34)

3. Why do you think Jesus prayed? (1:35-1:39)

4. What kind of attitude did Jesus have toward the leper? (1:40-1:45)

Take a moment to reread this section.

1. What is one question you have from Day 2?

2. What is one phrase or idea that catches your attention or speaks to you from Day 2?

3. In a word or a short phrase, what is one thing you learned about Jesus from Day 2?

4. Based on what has happened in your life in the last 24 hours, why do you think God had you read this today?

Day 3 Readings

Healing and Forgiving a Paralytic

2:1 Now after some days, when he returned to Capernaum, the news spread that he was at home. 2:2 So many gathered that there was no longer any room, not even by the door, and he preached the word to them. 2:3 Some people came bringing to him a paralytic, carried by four of them. 2:4 When they were not able to bring him in because of the crowd, they removed the roof above Jesus. Then, after tearing it out, they lowered the stretcher the paralytic was lying on. 2:5 When Jesus saw their faith, he said to the paralytic, "Son, your sins are forgiven." 2:6 Now some of the experts in the law were sitting there, turning these things over in their minds: 2:7 "Why does this man speak this way? He is blaspheming! Who can forgive sins but God alone?" 2:8 Now immediately, when Jesus realized in his spirit that they were contemplating such thoughts, he said to them, "Why are you thinking such things in your hearts? 2:9 Which is easier, to say to the paralytic, 'Your sins are forgiven,' or to say, 'Stand up, take your stretcher, and walk'? 2:10 But so that you may know that the Son of Man has authority on earth to forgive sins," – he said to the paralytic – 2:11 "I tell you, stand up, take your stretcher, and go home." 2:12 And immediately the man stood up, took his stretcher, and went out in front of them all. They were all amazed and glorified God, saying, "We have never seen anything like this!"

Faith (2:5) Belief, trust, and risk all mixed into one
Sins (2:5) Living our own way rather than God's way
Experts in the Law (2:6) People who studied the Old Testament carefully
Blaspheming (2:7) Speaking against someone, slander, curse

Day 3 Questions

The ultimate miracle is Jesus forgiving our sin.

1. Why do you think so many people gathered to hear Jesus teach? (2:1-2:2)

2. This paralytic had four very devoted friends who were even willing to tear a roof out. Who are your four best friends? Who are you a best friend to in your life? (2:3-2:4)

3. Do you think they believed Jesus when he first said, "Son, your sins are forgiven"? Why? (2:5-2:8)

4. How would you answer the question Jesus asked, "Which is easier, to say to the paralytic, 'Your sins are forgiven', or to say, 'Stand up, take your stretcher, and walk'"? Therefore why did he then heal that man? (2:9-2:12)

Take a moment to reread this section.

1. What is one question you have from Day 3?

2. What is one phrase or idea that catches your attention or speaks to you from Day 3?

3. In a word or a short phrase, what is one thing you learned about Jesus from Day 3?

4. Based on what has happened in your life in the last 24 hours, why do you think God had you read this today?

Day 4 Reading

The Call of Levi; Eating with Sinners

2:13 Jesus went out again by the sea. The whole crowd came to him, and he taught them. 2:14 As he went along, he saw Levi, the son of Alphaeus, sitting at the tax booth. "Follow me," he said to him. And he got up and followed him. 2:15 As Jesus was having a meal in Levi's home, many tax collectors and sinners were eating with Jesus and his disciples, for there were many who followed him. 2:16 When the experts in the law and the Pharisees saw that he was eating with sinners and tax collectors, they said to his disciples, "Why does he eat with tax collectors and sinners?" 2:17 When Jesus heard this he said to them, "Those who are healthy don't need a physician, but those who are sick do. I have not come to call the righteous, but sinners."

The Superiority of the New

2:18 Now John's disciples and the Pharisees were fasting. So they came to Jesus and said, "Why do the disciples of John and the disciples of the Pharisees fast, but your disciples don't fast?" 2:19 Jesus said to them, "The wedding guests cannot fast while the bridegroom is with them, can they? As long as they have the bridegroom with them they do not fast. 2:20 But the days are coming when the bridegroom will be taken from them, and at that time they will fast. 2:21 No one sews a patch of unshrunk cloth on an old garment; otherwise, the patch pulls away from it, the new from the old, and the tear becomes worse. 2:22 And no one pours new wine into old wineskins; otherwise, the wine will burst the skins, and both the wine and the skins will be destroyed. Instead new wine is poured into new wineskins."

Lord of the Sabbath

2:23 Jesus was going through the grain fields on a Sabbath, and his disciples began to pick some heads of wheat as they made their way. 2:24 So the Pharisees said to him, "Look, why are they doing what is against the law on the Sabbath?" 2:25 He said to them, "Have you never read what David did when he was in need and he and his companions were hungry – 2:26 how he entered the house of God when Abiathar was high priest and ate the sacred bread, which is against the law for any but the priests to eat, and also gave it to his companions?" 2:27 Then he said to them, "The Sabbath was made for people, not people for the Sabbath. 2:28 For this reason the Son of Man is lord even of the Sabbath."

Pharisees (2:16) Influential group of Jews who sought to observe every law in the Old Testament
Fasting (2:18) Abstaining from something to focus on God, often not eating food

Day 4 Questions

Jesus came to show the true heart of God, not just to maintain what everyone expected in his culture. He was a true revolutionary!

1. Jesus' simple instruction to a corrupt tax collector was simply, "Follow me". Of all the things Jesus could have said to a notorious sinner, why do you think he said this? (2:13-15)

2. How would you answer the religious leaders' question, "Why does [Jesus] eat with tax collectors and sinners?" (2:16-2:17)

3. Jesus' examples of cloth and wine are meant to show that the people needed to be open to a different understanding of God than they expected. As you've learned more about God, what has changed in your understanding? (2:18-2:22)

4. Sabbath is Saturday, the traditional day of rest for Jewish people. How is it possible that a great teaching can be twisted into something it wasn't meant to be?

Take a moment to reread this section.

1. What is one question you have from Day 4?

2. What is one phrase or idea that catches your attention or speaks to you from Day 4?

3. In a word or a short phrase, what is one thing you learned about Jesus from Day 4?

4. Based on what has happened in your life in the last 24 hours, why do you think God had you read this today?

Day 5 Reading

Healing a Withered Hand

3:1 Then Jesus entered the synagogue again, and a man was there who had a withered hand. 3:2 They watched Jesus closely to see if he would heal him on the Sabbath, so that they could accuse him. 3:3 So he said to the man who had the withered hand, "Stand up among all these people." 3:4 Then he said to them, "Is it lawful to do good on the Sabbath, or evil, to save a life or destroy it?" But they were silent. 3:5 After looking around at them in anger, grieved by the hardness of their hearts, he said to the man, "Stretch out your hand." He stretched it out, and his hand was restored. 3:6 So the Pharisees went out immediately and began plotting with the Herodians, as to how they could assassinate him.

Crowds by the Sea

3:7 Then Jesus went away with his disciples to the sea, and a great multitude from Galilee followed him. And from Judea, 3:8 Jerusalem, Idumea, beyond the Jordan River, and around Tyre and Sidon a great multitude came to him when they heard about the things he had done. 3:9 Because of the crowd, he told his disciples to have a small boat ready for him so the crowd would not press toward him. 3:10 For he had healed many, so that all who were afflicted with diseases pressed toward him in order to touch him. 3:11 And whenever the unclean spirits saw him, they fell down before him and cried out, "You are the Son of God." 3:12 But he sternly ordered them not to make him known.

Appointing the Twelve Apostles

3:13 Now Jesus went up the mountain and called for those he wanted, and they came to him. 3:14 He appointed twelve (whom he named apostles), so that they would be with him and he could send them to preach 3:15 and to have authority to cast out demons. 3:16 He appointed twelve: To Simon he gave the name Peter; 3:17 to James and his brother John, the sons of Zebedee, he gave the name Boanerges (that is, "sons of thunder"); 3:18 and Andrew, Philip, Bartholomew, Matthew, Thomas, James the son of Alphaeus, Thaddaeus, Simon the Zealot, 3:19 and Judas Iscariot, who betrayed him.

Herodians (3:6) A group of people connected with government leader Herod and the Pharisees
Disciples (3:7) Close followers who wanted to learn the ways of Jesus
Unclean Spirits (3:11) Demonic spirits
Apostles (3:14) A person, or group of people, sent out for a particular task

Day 5 Questions

The self-righteous people worked to assassinate Jesus. The needy people worked to be close to Jesus. How do you see yourself today?

1. How do you think people could become so hard-hearted to not want to see people's lives healed and instead want to assassinate Jesus? (3:1-3:6)

2. The people in Jesus' day who were afflicted with diseases and all kinds of problems surrounded Jesus and pressed toward him. Do people do this today? Why or why not? (3:7-3:12)

3. Why did Jesus choose Judas, who Jesus knew would betray him, to follow him? (3:13-3:19)

Take a moment to reread this section.

1. What is one question you have from Day 5?

2. What is one phrase or idea that catches your attention or speaks to you from Day 5?

3. In a word or a short phrase, what is one thing you learned about Jesus from Day 5?

4. Based on what has happened in your life in the last 24 hours, why do you think God had you read this today?

Day 6 Reading

Jesus and Beelzebul

3:20 Now Jesus went home, and a crowd gathered so that they were not able to eat. 3:21 When his family heard this they went out to restrain him, for they said, "He is out of his mind." 3:22 The experts in the law who came down from Jerusalem said, "He is possessed by Beelzebul," and, "By the ruler of demons he casts out demons." 3:23 So he called them and spoke to them in parables: "How can Satan cast out Satan? 3:24 If a kingdom is divided against itself, that kingdom will not be able to stand. 3:25 If a house is divided against itself, that house will not be able to stand. 3:26 And if Satan rises against himself and is divided, he is not able to stand and his end has come. 3:27 But no one is able to enter a strong man's house and steal his property unless he first ties up the strong man. Then he can thoroughly plunder his house. 3:28 I tell you the truth, people will be forgiven for all sins, even all the blasphemies they utter. 3:29 But whoever blasphemes against the Holy Spirit will never be forgiven, but is guilty of an eternal sin" 3:30 (because they said, "He has an unclean spirit").

Jesus' True Family

3:31 Then Jesus' mother and his brothers came. Standing outside, they sent word to him, to summon him. 3:32 A crowd was sitting around him and they said to him, "Look, your mother and your brothers are outside looking for you." 3:33 He answered them and said, "Who are my mother and my brothers?" 3:34 And looking at those who were sitting around him in a circle, he said, "Here are my mother and my brothers! 3:35 For whoever does the will of God is my brother and sister and mother."

Beelzebub (3:22) Prince of demons, Satan
Blasphemies Against the Holy Spirit (3:29) Lying about God, basically denying God

Day 6 Questions

When we believe and live for Jesus it will be good news for some of our friends and hard news for other friends.

1. Jesus' teaching was radical and when he went to his home town they had a hard time understanding him. Why is it hard for people to accept a person when this person starts acting differently? (3:20-3:27)

2. Every sin can be forgiven by Jesus if you believe in him. Why do you think the Bible says you cannot be forgiven if you say Jesus has an "unclean spirit"? (3:28-3:30)

3. Why do you think Jesus teaches that he is family to those who do God's will? (3:31-3:35)

Take a moment to reread this section.

1. What is one question you have from Day 6?

2. What is one phrase or idea that catches your attention or speaks to you from Day 6?

3. In a word or a short phrase, what is one thing you learned about Jesus from Day 6?

4. Based on what has happened in your life in the last 24 hours, why do you think God had you read this today?

Day 7 Reading

The Parable of the Sower

4:1 Again he began to teach by the lake. Such a large crowd gathered around him that he got into a boat on the lake and sat there while the whole crowd was on the shore by the lake. 4:2 He taught them many things in parables, and in his teaching said to them: 4:3 "Listen! A sower went out to sow. 4:4 And as he sowed, some seed fell along the path, and the birds came and devoured it. 4:5 Other seed fell on rocky ground where it did not have much soil. It sprang up at once because the soil was not deep. 4:6 When the sun came up it was scorched, and because it did not have sufficient root, it withered. 4:7 Other seed fell among the thorns, and they grew up and choked it, and it did not produce grain. 4:8 But other seed fell on good soil and produced grain, sprouting and growing; some yielded thirty times as much, some sixty, and some a hundred times." 4:9 And he said, "Whoever has ears to hear had better listen!"

The Purpose of Parables

4:10 When he was alone, those around him with the twelve asked him about the parables. 4:11 He said to them, "The secret of the kingdom of God has been given to you. But to those outside, everything is in parables,
> 4:12 so that although they look they may look but not see,
> and although they hear they may hear but not understand,
> so they may not repent and be forgiven."

4:13 He said to them, "Don't you understand this parable? Then how will you understand any parable? 4:14 The sower sows the word. 4:15 These are the ones on the path where the word is sown: Whenever they hear, immediately Satan comes and snatches the word that was sown in them. 4:16 These are the ones sown on rocky ground: As soon as they hear the word, they receive it with joy. 4:17 But they have no root in themselves and do not endure. Then, when trouble or persecution comes because of the word, immediately they fall away. 4:18 Others are the ones sown among thorns: They are those who hear the word, 4:19 but worldly cares, the seductiveness of wealth, and the desire for other things come in and choke the word, and it produces nothing. 4:20 But these are the ones sown on good soil: They hear the word and receive it and bear fruit, one thirty times as much, one sixty, and one a hundred."

Parables (4:2) _Short story with a purpose or double meaning_
Kingdom of God (4:11) _A place where God is king_

Day 7 Questions

Jesus wants to make it clear that those who hear God's word, receive it, and put it into practice will see 30, 60 or even 100 times what they put into it.

1. Why do you think Jesus spoke in parables? Is the first part of this parable hard to understand? (4:1-12)

2. Why do you think two people can hear the same teaching from Jesus and it can impact them so differently? (4:10-13)

3. What are the four types of soils? What is the outcome of each? (4:14-20)

4. Which soil most closely resembles your situation right now? (4:14-20)

Take a moment to reread this section.

1. What is one question you have from Day 7?

2. What is one phrase or idea that catches your attention or speaks to you from Day 7?

3. In a word or a short phrase, what is one thing you learned about Jesus from Day 7?

4. Based on what has happened in your life in the last 24 hours, why do you think God had you read this today?

Day 8 Reading

The Parable of the Lamp

4:21 He also said to them, "A lamp isn't brought to be put under a basket or under a bed, is it? Isn't it to be placed on a lampstand? 4:22 For nothing is hidden except to be revealed, and nothing concealed except to be brought to light. 4:23 If anyone has ears to hear, he had better listen!" 4:24 And he said to them, "Take care about what you hear. The measure you use will be the measure you receive, and more will be added to you. 4:25 For whoever has will be given more, but whoever does not have, even what he has will be taken from him."

The Parable of the Growing Seed

4:26 He also said, "The kingdom of God is like someone who spreads seed on the ground. 4:27 He goes to sleep and gets up, night and day, and the seed sprouts and grows, though he does not know how. 4:28 By itself the soil produces a crop, first the stalk, then the head, then the full grain in the head. 4:29 And when the grain is ripe, he sends in the sickle because the harvest has come."

The Parable of the Mustard Seed

4:30 He also asked, "To what can we compare the kingdom of God, or what parable can we use to present it? 4:31 It is like a mustard seed that when sown in the ground, even though it is the smallest of all the seeds in the ground – 4:32 when it is sown, it grows up, becomes the greatest of all garden plants, and grows large branches so that the wild birds can nest in its shade."

The Use of Parables

4:33 So with many parables like these, he spoke the word to them, as they were able to hear. 4:34 He did not speak to them without a parable. But privately he explained everything to his own disciples.

Stilling of a Storm

4:35 On that day, when evening came, Jesus said to his disciples, "Let's go across to the other side of the lake." 4:36 So after leaving the crowd, they took him along, just as he was, in the boat, and other boats were with him. 4:37 Now a great windstorm developed and the waves were breaking into the boat, so that the boat was nearly swamped. 4:38 But he was in the stern, sleeping on a cushion. They woke him up and said to him, "Teacher, don't you care that we are about to die?" 4:39 So he got up and rebuked the wind, and said to the sea, "Be quiet! Calm down!" Then the wind stopped, and it was dead calm. 4:40 And he said to them, "Why are you cowardly? Do you still not have faith?" 4:41 They were overwhelmed by fear and said to one another, "Who then is this? Even the wind and sea obey him!"

Day 8 Questions

God can work in anyone whether you have faith as small as a mustard seed or feel like a coward. Pay attention to what you hear. Put it into practice and you will be given even more.

1. Why do you think Jesus puts such a high priority on listening carefully to His teaching? (4:21-25)

2. A mustard seed starts very small and then can become one of the largest plants. Why do you think Jesus compares it to the kingdom of God which is God's work through us here on earth? (4:30-32)

3. Jesus tells the disciples to not be "cowardly" but to have faith. What are some areas you are "cowardly" or lack faith in your life right now? (4:35-41)

Take a moment to reread this section.

1. What is one question you have from Day 8?

2. What is one phrase or idea that catches your attention or speaks to you from Day 8?

3. In a word or a short phrase, what is one thing you learned about Jesus from Day 8?

4. Based on what has happened in your life in the last 24 hours, why do you think God had you read this today?

Day 9 Reading

Healing of a Demoniac

5:1 So they came to the other side of the lake, to the region of the Gerasenes. 5:2 Just as Jesus was getting out of the boat, a man with an unclean spirit came from the tombs and met him. 5:3 He lived among the tombs, and no one could bind him anymore, not even with a chain. 5:4 For his hands and feet had often been bound with chains and shackles, but he had torn the chains apart and broken the shackles in pieces. No one was strong enough to subdue him. 5:5 Each night and every day among the tombs and in the mountains, he would cry out and cut himself with stones. 5:6 When he saw Jesus from a distance, he ran and bowed down before him. 5:7 Then he cried out with a loud voice, "Leave me alone, Jesus, Son of the Most High God! I implore you by God – do not torment me!" 5:8 (For Jesus had said to him, "Come out of that man, you unclean spirit!") 5:9 Jesus asked him, "What is your name?" And he said, "My name is Legion, for we are many." 5:10 He begged Jesus repeatedly not to send them out of the region. 5:11 There on the hillside, a great herd of pigs was feeding. 5:12 And the demonic spirits begged him, "Send us into the pigs. Let us enter them." 5:13 Jesus gave them permission. So the unclean spirits came out and went into the pigs. Then the herd rushed down the steep slope into the lake, and about two thousand were drowned in the lake.

5:14 Now the herdsmen ran off and spread the news in the town and countryside, and the people went out to see what had happened. 5:15 They came to Jesus and saw the demon-possessed man sitting there, clothed and in his right mind – the one who had the "Legion" – and they were afraid. 5:16 Those who had seen what had happened to the demon-possessed man reported it, and they also told about the pigs. 5:17 Then they asked Jesus to leave their region. 5:18 As he was getting into the boat the man who had been demon-possessed asked if he could go with him. 5:19 But Jesus did not permit him to do so. Instead, he said to him, "Go to your home and to your people and tell them what the Lord has done for you, that he had mercy on you." 5:20 So he went away and began to proclaim in the Decapolis what Jesus had done for him, and all were amazed.

———

Legion (5:9) A division of an army with 4000-6000 soldiers
Decapolis (5:20) 10 specific cities

Day 9 Questions

Evil exists, but it bows down at the feet of Jesus. All power belongs to God.

1. Do you think there are demonic influences in the world like the one Jesus encountered? Why? (5:1-6)

2. Why do you think the man who was unclean, lived among tombs, broke chains, could not be bound, cried out at morning and night, cut himself…would run and bow down before Jesus? (5:3-6)

3. Why do you think Jesus told the man to go home and tell his people what the Lord has done for him? (5:18-20)

Take a moment to reread this section.

1. What is one question you have from Day 9?

2. What is one phrase or idea that catches your attention or speaks to you from Day 9?

3. In a word or a short phrase, what is one thing you learned about Jesus from Day 9?

4. Based on what has happened in your life in the last 24 hours, why do you think God had you read this today?

Day 10 Reading

Restoration and Healing

5:21 When Jesus had crossed again in a boat to the other side, a large crowd gathered around him, and he was by the sea. 5:22 Then one of the synagogue rulers, named Jairus, came up, and when he saw Jesus, he fell at his feet. 5:23 He asked him urgently, "My little daughter is near death. Come and lay your hands on her so that she may be healed and live." 5:24 Jesus went with him, and a large crowd followed and pressed around him.

5:25 Now a woman was there who had been suffering from a hemorrhage for twelve years. 5:26 She had endured a great deal under the care of many doctors and had spent all that she had. Yet instead of getting better, she grew worse. 5:27 When she heard about Jesus, she came up behind him in the crowd and touched his cloak, 5:28 for she kept saying, "If only I touch his clothes, I will be healed." 5:29 At once the bleeding stopped, and she felt in her body that she was healed of her disease. 5:30 Jesus knew at once that power had gone out from him. He turned around in the crowd and said, "Who touched my clothes?" 5:31 His disciples said to him, "You see the crowd pressing against you and you say, 'Who touched me?'" 5:32 But he looked around to see who had done it. 5:33 Then the woman, with fear and trembling, knowing what had happened to her, came and fell down before him and told him the whole truth. 5:34 He said to her, "Daughter, your faith has made you well. Go in peace, and be healed of your disease."

5:35 While he was still speaking, people came from the synagogue ruler's house saying, "Your daughter has died. Why trouble the teacher any longer?" 5:36 But Jesus, paying no attention to what was said, told the synagogue ruler, "Do not be afraid; just believe." 5:37 He did not let anyone follow him except Peter, James, and John, the brother of James. 5:38 They came to the house of the synagogue ruler where he saw noisy confusion and people weeping and wailing loudly. 5:39 When he entered he said to them, "Why are you distressed and weeping? The child is not dead but asleep." 5:40 And they began making fun of him. But he put them all outside and he took the child's father and mother and his own companions and went into the room where the child was. 5:41 Then, gently taking the child by the hand, he said to her, "*Talitha koum,*" which means, "Little girl, I say to you, get up." 5:42 The girl got up at once and began to walk around (she was twelve years old). They were completely astonished at this. 5:43 He strictly ordered that no one should know about this, and told them to give her something to eat.

Day 10 Questions

Whether you are an important ruler or someone overlooked by everyone, it only takes one touch from Jesus to change your life.

1. What does it tell you about Jesus that an important ruler "fell" at Jesus' feet? (5:21-24)

2. After twelve years of incurable suffering, why do you think the woman snuck in to touch Jesus? (5:25-34)

3. What does verse 34 say that made the bleeding woman well? Why do you think this is the key to the change in her life? (5:25-34)

4. Why do you think Jesus told the people, "Do not be afraid; just believe"?

Take a moment to reread this section.

1. What is one question you have from Day 10?

2. What is one phrase or idea that catches your attention or speaks to you from Day 10?

3. In a word or a short phrase, what is one thing you learned about Jesus from Day 10?

4. Based on what has happened in your life in the last 24 hours, why do you think God had you read this today?

Rejection at Nazareth

6:1 Now Jesus left that place and came to his hometown, and his disciples followed him. 6:2 When the Sabbath came, he began to teach in the synagogue. Many who heard him were astonished, saying, "Where did he get these ideas? And what is this wisdom that has been given to him? What are these miracles that are done through his hands? 6:3 Isn't this the carpenter, the son of Mary and brother of James, Joses, Judas, and Simon? And aren't his sisters here with us?" And so they took offense at him. 6:4 Then Jesus said to them, "A prophet is not without honor except in his hometown, and among his relatives, and in his own house." 6:5 He was not able to do a miracle there, except to lay his hands on a few sick people and heal them. 6:6 And he was amazed because of their unbelief. Then he went around among the villages and taught.

Sending Out the Twelve Apostles

6:7 Jesus called the twelve and began to send them out two by two. He gave them authority over the unclean spirits. 6:8 He instructed them to take nothing for the journey except a staff – no bread, no bag, no money in their belts – 6:9 and to put on sandals but not to wear two tunics. 6:10 He said to them, "Wherever you enter a house, stay there until you leave the area. 6:11 If a place will not welcome you or listen to you, as you go out from there, shake the dust off your feet as a testimony against them." 6:12 So they went out and preached that all should repent. 6:13 They cast out many demons and anointed many sick people with oil and healed them.

The Death of John the Baptist

6:14 Now King Herod heard this, for Jesus' name had become known. Some were saying, "John the baptizer has been raised from the dead, and because of this, miraculous powers are at work in him." 6:15 Others said, "He is Elijah." Others said, "He is a prophet, like one of the prophets from the past." 6:16 But when Herod heard this, he said, "John, whom I beheaded, has been raised!" 6:17 For Herod himself had sent men, arrested John, and bound him in prison on account of Herodias, his brother Philip's wife, because Herod had married her. 6:18 For John had repeatedly told Herod, "It is not lawful for you to have your brother's wife." 6:19 So Herodias nursed a grudge against him and wanted to kill him. But she could not 6:20 because Herod stood in awe of John and protected him, since he knew that John was a righteous and holy man. When Herod heard him, he was thoroughly baffled, and yet he liked to listen to John.

6:21 But a suitable day came, when Herod gave a banquet on his birthday for his court officials, military commanders, and leaders of Galilee. 6:22 When his daughter Herodias came in and danced, she pleased Herod and his dinner guests. The king said to the girl, "Ask me for whatever you want and I will give it to you." 6:23 He swore to her, "Whatever you ask I will give you, up to half my kingdom." 6:24 So she went out and said to her mother, "What should I ask for?" Her mother said, "The head of John the baptizer." 6:25 Immediately she hurried back to the king and made her request: "I want the head of John the Baptist on a platter immediately." 6:26 Although it grieved the king deeply, he did not want to reject her request because of his oath and his guests. 6:27 So the king sent an executioner at once to bring John's head, and he went and beheaded John in prison. 6:28 He brought his head on a platter and gave it to the girl, and the girl gave it to her mother. 6:29 When John's disciples heard this, they came and took his body and placed it in a tomb.

Day 11 Questions

Jesus was misunderstood by nearly everyone he encountered. Christians should strive to live like Jesus and also expect to be misunderstood at times too.

1. Jesus' neighbors and hometown had a hard time accepting him. Why do you think this happened? (6:1-6)

2. When Jesus sent people out, he sent them in groups of two. Why do you think Jesus paired people together? Who do you depend on as a partner in your life? (6:7-12)

3. John the Baptist paid the ultimate price, his life, for standing up for what is right. Why do you think they compared Jesus to him? To what extent should we be willing to take a stand for right and wrong? (6:14-29)

Take a moment to reread this section.

1. What is one question you have from Day 11?

2. What is one phrase or idea that catches your attention or speaks to you from Day 11?

3. In a word or a short phrase, what is one thing you learned about Jesus from Day 11?

4. Based on what has happened in your life in the last 24 hours, why do you think God had you read this today?

Day 12 Reading

The Feeding of the Five Thousand

6:30 Then the apostles gathered around Jesus and told him everything they had done and taught. 6:31 He said to them, "Come with me privately to an isolated place and rest a while" (for many were coming and going, and there was no time to eat). 6:32 So they went away by themselves in a boat to some remote place. 6:33 But many saw them leaving and recognized them, and they hurried on foot from all the towns and arrived there ahead of them. 6:34 As Jesus came ashore he saw the large crowd and he had compassion on them, because they were like sheep without a shepherd. So he taught them many things.

6:35 When it was already late, his disciples came to him and said, "This is an isolated place and it is already very late. 6:36 Send them away so that they can go into the surrounding countryside and villages and buy something for themselves to eat." 6:37 But he answered them, "You give them something to eat." And they said, "Should we go and buy bread for two hundred silver coins and give it to them to eat?" 6:38 He said to them, "How many loaves do you have? Go and see." When they found out, they said, "Five – and two fish." 6:39 Then he directed them all to sit down in groups on the green grass. 6:40 So they reclined in groups of hundreds and fifties. 6:41 He took the five loaves and the two fish, and looking up to heaven, he gave thanks and broke the loaves. He gave them to his disciples to serve the people, and he divided the two fish among them all. 6:42 They all ate and were satisfied, 6:43 and they picked up the broken pieces and fish that were left over, twelve baskets full. 6:44 Now there were five thousand men who ate the bread.

Walking on Water

6:45 Immediately Jesus made his disciples get into the boat and go on ahead to the other side, to Bethsaida, while he dispersed the crowd. 6:46 After saying good-bye to them, he went to the mountain to pray. 6:47 When evening came, the boat was in the middle of the sea and he was alone on the land. 6:48 He saw them straining at the oars, because the wind was against them. As the night was ending, he came to them walking on the sea, for he wanted to pass by them. 6:49 When they saw him walking on the water they thought he was a ghost. They cried out, 6:50 for they all saw him and were terrified. But immediately he spoke to them: "Have courage! It is I. Do not be afraid." 6:51 Then he went up with them into the boat, and the wind ceased. They were completely astonished, 6:52 because they did not understand about the loaves, but their hearts were hardened.

Healing the Sick

6:53 After they had crossed over, they came to land at Gennesaret and anchored there. 6:54 As they got out of the boat, people immediately recognized Jesus. 6:55 They ran through that whole region and began to bring the sick on mats to wherever he was rumored to be. 6:56 And wherever he would go – into villages, towns, or countryside – they would place the sick in the marketplaces, and would ask him if they could just touch the edge of his cloak, and all who touched it were healed.

Day 12 Questions

Whether Jesus is miraculously creating food, walking on water, or healing people, He is showing His power as God in the flesh. Where do you need God's power today?

1. In today's terms, how would you paraphrase people who are "sheep without a shepherd"? Why does Jesus have compassion on them? (6:30-34)

2. Why do you think Jesus asked the disciples to feed the people, knowing full well they didn't have enough food? (6:35-44)

3. Is there an area in your life where hearing these words from God would help: "Have courage. It is I. Do not be afraid"? If so, describe. (6:45-52)

4. If even touching the edge of Jesus' clothes healed people, what does this tell us about Jesus' power? How have you experienced Jesus' power in your life? (6:53-56)

Take a moment to reread this section.

1. What is one question you have from Day 12?

2. What is one phrase or idea that catches your attention or speaks to you from Day 12?

3. In a word or a short phrase, what is one thing you learned about Jesus from Day 12?

4. Based on what has happened in your life in the last 24 hours, why do you think God had you read this today?

Day 13 Reading

Breaking Human Traditions

7:1 Now the Pharisees and some of the experts in the law who came from Jerusalem gathered around him. 7:2 And they saw that some of Jesus' disciples ate their bread with unclean hands, that is, unwashed. 7:3 (For the Pharisees and all the Jews do not eat unless they perform a ritual washing, holding fast to the tradition of the elders. 7:4 And when they come from the marketplace, they do not eat unless they wash. They hold fast to many other traditions: the washing of cups, pots, kettles, and dining couches.) 7:5 The Pharisees and the experts in the law asked him, "Why do your disciples not live according to the tradition of the elders, but eat with unwashed hands?" 7:6 He said to them, "Isaiah prophesied correctly about you hypocrites, as it is written:

'This people honors me with their lips,
but their heart is far from me.
7:7 *They worship me in vain,*
teaching as doctrine the commandments of men.'

7:8 Having no regard for the command of God, you hold fast to human tradition." 7:9 He also said to them, "You neatly reject the commandment of God in order to set up your tradition. 7:10 For Moses said, '*Honor your father and your mother,*' and, '*Whoever insults his father or mother must be put to death.*' 7:11 But you say that if anyone tells his father or mother, 'Whatever help you would have received from me is *corban*' (that is, a gift for God), 7:12 then you no longer permit him to do anything for his father or mother. 7:13 Thus you nullify the word of God by your tradition that you have handed down. And you do many things like this."

7:14 Then he called the crowd again and said to them, "Listen to me, everyone, and understand. 7:15 There is nothing outside of a person that can defile him by going into him. Rather, it is what comes out of a person that defiles him."

7:17 Now when Jesus had left the crowd and entered the house, his disciples asked him about the parable. 7:18 He said to them, "Are you so foolish? Don't you understand that whatever goes into a person from outside cannot defile him? 7:19 For it does not enter his heart but his stomach, and then goes out into the sewer." (This means all foods are clean.) 7:20 He said, "What comes out of a person defiles him. 7:21 For from within, out of the human heart, come evil ideas, sexual immorality, theft, murder, 7:22 adultery, greed, evil, deceit, debauchery, envy, slander, pride, and folly. 7:23 All these evils come from within and defile a person."

Hypocrite (7:6) Pretender, play-actor, insincere

Day 13 Questions

Jesus' focus is not on what people can see in you, but on what only He can see in you.

1. Why does Jesus criticize people whose words don't match their hearts? (7:1-6)

2. How can one be certain if a teaching is from God or man? (7:7)

3. Based on Jesus' teaching what is more dangerous...the sin that is "out there" or the sin that is "in us"? Why? (7:8-22)

Take a moment to reread this section.

1. What is one question you have from Day 13?

2. What is one phrase or idea that catches your attention or speaks to you from Day 13?

3. In a word or a short phrase, what is one thing you learned about Jesus from Day 13?

4. Based on what has happened in your life in the last 24 hours, why do you think God had you read this today?

Day 14 Reading

A Syrophoenician Woman's Faith

7:24 After Jesus left there, he went to the region of Tyre. When he went into a house, he did not want anyone to know, but he was not able to escape notice. 7:25 Instead, a woman whose young daughter had an unclean spirit immediately heard about him and came and fell at his feet. 7:26 The woman was a Greek, of Syrophoenician origin. She asked him to cast the demon out of her daughter. 7:27 He said to her, "Let the children be satisfied first, for it is not right to take the children's bread and to throw it to the dogs." 7:28 She answered, "Yes, Lord, but even the dogs under the table eat the children's crumbs." 7:29 Then he said to her, "Because you said this, you may go. The demon has left your daughter." 7:30 She went home and found the child lying on the bed, and the demon gone.

Healing a Deaf Mute

7:31 Then Jesus went out again from the region of Tyre and came through Sidon to the Sea of Galilee in the region of the Decapolis. 7:32 They brought to him a deaf man who had difficulty speaking, and they asked him to place his hands on him. 7:33 After Jesus took him aside privately, away from the crowd, he put his fingers in the man's ears, and after spitting, he touched his tongue. 7:34 Then he looked up to heaven and said with a sigh, "*Ephphatha*" (that is, "Be opened"). 7:35 And immediately the man's ears were opened, his tongue loosened, and he spoke plainly. 7:36 Jesus ordered them not to tell anything. But as much as he ordered them not to do this, they proclaimed it all the more. 7:37 People were completely astounded and said, "He has done everything well. He even makes the deaf hear and the mute speak."

Syrophoenician (7:26) A person from Phoenicia, an area in Syria, this woman was not Jewish

Day 14 Questions

Jesus is God and has the power to do what He wants. Don't be afraid to fall at His feet and keep on asking questions.

1. Make a list of things that you would be willing to "fall at the feet" of Jesus for help. (7:24-25)

2. At first Jesus does not grant the woman's wish, but He does grant her request when she doesn't give up. What does this teach us about making our requests to God? (7:26-30)

3. Why do you think people disobeyed Jesus and kept telling others about him? (7:31-36)

4. People were saying, "He has done everything well." What are some things that Jesus has done well in your life? (7:37)

Take a moment to reread this section.

1. What is one question you have from Day 14?

2. What is one phrase or idea that catches your attention or speaks to you from Day 14?

3. In a word or a short phrase, what is one thing you learned about Jesus from Day 14?

4. Based on what has happened in your life in the last 24 hours, why do you think God had you read this today?

Day 15 Reading

The Feeding of the Four Thousand

8:1 In those days there was another large crowd with nothing to eat. So Jesus called his disciples and said to them, 8:2 "I have compassion on the crowd, because they have already been here with me three days, and they have nothing to eat. 8:3 If I send them home hungry, they will faint on the way, and some of them have come from a great distance." 8:4 His disciples answered him, "Where can someone get enough bread in this desolate place to satisfy these people?" 8:5 He asked them, "How many loaves do you have?" They replied, "Seven." 8:6 Then he directed the crowd to sit down on the ground. After he took the seven loaves and gave thanks, he broke them and began giving them to the disciples to serve. So they served the crowd. 8:7 They also had a few small fish. After giving thanks for these, he told them to serve these as well. 8:8 Everyone ate and was satisfied, and they picked up the broken pieces left over, seven baskets full. 8:9 There were about four thousand who ate. Then he dismissed them. 8:10 Immediately he got into a boat with his disciples and went to the district of Dalmanutha.

The Demand for a Sign

8:11 Then the Pharisees came and began to argue with Jesus, asking for a sign from heaven to test him. 8:12 Sighing deeply in his spirit he said, "Why does this generation look for a sign? I tell you the truth, no sign will be given to this generation." 8:13 Then he left them, got back into the boat, and went to the other side.

The Yeast of the Pharisees and Herod

8:14 Now they had forgotten to take bread, except for one loaf they had with them in the boat. 8:15 And Jesus ordered them, "Watch out! Beware of the yeast of the Pharisees and the yeast of Herod!" 8:16 So they began to discuss with one another about having no bread. 8:17 When he learned of this, Jesus said to them, "Why are you arguing about having no bread? Do you still not see or understand? Have your hearts been hardened? 8:18 Though you have eyes, don't you see? And though you have ears, can't you hear? Don't you remember? 8:19 When I broke the five loaves for the five thousand, how many baskets full of pieces did you pick up?" They replied, "Twelve." 8:20 "When I broke the seven loaves for the four thousand, how many baskets full of pieces did you pick up?" They replied, "Seven." 8:21 Then he said to them, "Do you still not understand?"

Yeast (8:15) A small ingredient that makes bread rise, a metaphor for corruption that works through something or someone

Day 1 5 Questions

We are all prone to forget the miracles Jesus has done in our past. Take a moment to think of a few. This will help you have faith for the challenges of today.

1. If Jesus knew that there was no food and that more food was too far away, do you think he had the miracle already planned? If so, what does this say about our hard situations? (8:1-10)

2. How long do you think it took for the disciples to realize God's solution to their hunger? Keep in mind that Jesus had just fed 5000 people in Mark 6:30-44. (8:1-10)

3. Why do you think Jesus would not give the Pharisees a "sign" when he had just done an incredible miracle for the people? (8:11-13)

4. Yeast spreads quickly through dough. What do you think Jesus was saying when he said, "Beware of the yeast of the Pharisees"? (8:14-21)

Take a moment to reread this section.

1. What is one question you have from Day 15?

2. What is one phrase or idea that catches your attention or speaks to you from Day 15?

3. In a word or a short phrase, what is one thing you learned about Jesus from Day 15?

4. Based on what has happened in your life in the last 24 hours, why do you think God had you read this today?

A Two-stage Healing

8:22 Then they came to Bethsaida. They brought a blind man to Jesus and asked him to touch him. 8:23 He took the blind man by the hand and brought him outside of the village. Then he spit on his eyes, placed his hands on his eyes and asked, "Do you see anything?" 8:24 Regaining his sight he said, "I see people, but they look like trees walking." 8:25 Then Jesus placed his hands on the man's eyes again. And he opened his eyes, his sight was restored, and he saw everything clearly. 8:26 Jesus sent him home, saying, "Do not even go into the village."

Peter's Confession

8:27 Then Jesus and his disciples went to the villages of Caesarea Philippi. On the way he asked his disciples, "Who do people say that I am?" 8:28 They said, "John the Baptist, others say Elijah, and still others, one of the prophets." 8:29 He asked them, "But who do you say that I am?" Peter answered him, "You are the Christ." 8:30 Then he warned them not to tell anyone about him.

First Prediction of Jesus' Death and Resurrection

8:31 Then Jesus began to teach them that the Son of Man must suffer many things and be rejected by the elders, chief priests, and experts in the law, and be killed, and after three days rise again. 8:32 He spoke openly about this. So Peter took him aside and began to rebuke him. 8:33 But after turning and looking at his disciples, he rebuked Peter and said, "Get behind me, Satan. You are not setting your mind on God's interests, but on man's."

Following Jesus

8:34 Then Jesus called the crowd, along with his disciples, and said to them, "If anyone wants to become my follower, he must deny himself, take up his cross, and follow me. 8:35 For whoever wants to save his life will lose it, but whoever loses his life for my sake and for the gospel will save it. 8:36 For what benefit is it for a person to gain the whole world, yet forfeit his life? 8:37 What can a person give in exchange for his life? 8:38 For if anyone is ashamed of me and my words in this adulterous and sinful generation, the Son of Man will also be ashamed of him when he comes in the glory of his Father with the holy angels." 9:1 And he said to them, "I tell you the truth, there are some standing here who will not experience death before they see the kingdom of God come with power."

John the Baptist (8:28) See Mark 1:4, a contemporary of Jesus who emphasized repentance
Elijah (8:28) A prophet from the Old Testament who performed miracles around 900 B.C.

Day 16 Questions

When we set our mind and life on God's interests, we are on the path of following Jesus.

1. Jesus healed the man's sight so he could see clearly. What has God helped you to see more clearly in your life? (8:22-26)

2. What is the difference between asking: "what do people say?" and "what do you say?" Why do you think Jesus asks this question? (8:27-30)

3. Why do you think Peter wanted to "rebuke" Jesus? Have you ever wanted to do that? If so, why? (8:31-33)

4. What are Jesus' instructions for anyone who wants to be his follower? In your own words, explain what each part of his answer means. (8:34-9:1)

Take a moment to reread this section.

1. What is one question you have from Day 16?

2. What is one phrase or idea that catches your attention or speaks to you from Day 16?

3. In a word or a short phrase, what is one thing you learned about Jesus from Day 16?

4. Based on what has happened in your life in the last 24 hours, why do you think God had you read this today?

Day 17 Reading

The Transfiguration

9:2 Six days later Jesus took with him Peter, James, and John and led them alone up a high mountain privately. And he was transfigured before them, 9:3 and his clothes became radiantly white, more so than any launderer in the world could bleach them. 9:4 Then Elijah appeared before them along with Moses, and they were talking with Jesus. 9:5 So Peter said to Jesus, "Rabbi, it is good for us to be here. Let us make three shelters – one for you, one for Moses, and one for Elijah." 9:6 (For they were afraid, and he did not know what to say.) 9:7 Then a cloud overshadowed them, and a voice came from the cloud, "This is my one dear Son. Listen to him!" 9:8 Suddenly when they looked around, they saw no one with them any more except Jesus.

9:9 As they were coming down from the mountain, he gave them orders not to tell anyone what they had seen until after the Son of Man had risen from the dead. 9:10 They kept this statement to themselves, discussing what this rising from the dead meant.

9:11 Then they asked him, "Why do the experts in the law say that Elijah must come first?" 9:12 He said to them, "Elijah does indeed come first, and restores all things. And why is it written that the Son of Man must suffer many things and be despised? 9:13 But I tell you that Elijah has certainly come, and they did to him whatever they wanted, just as it is written about him."

The Disciples' Failure to Heal

9:14 When they came to the disciples, they saw a large crowd around them and experts in the law arguing with them. 9:15 When the whole crowd saw him, they were amazed and ran at once and greeted him. 9:16 He asked them, "What are you arguing about with them?" 9:17 A member of the crowd said to him, "Teacher, I brought you my son, who is possessed by a spirit that makes him mute. 9:18 Whenever it seizes him, it throws him down, and he foams at the mouth, grinds his teeth, and becomes rigid. I asked your disciples to cast it out, but they were not able to do so." 9:19 He answered them, "You unbelieving generation! How much longer must I be with you? How much longer must I endure you? Bring him to me." 9:20 So they brought the boy to him. When the spirit saw him, it immediately threw the boy into a convulsion. He fell on the ground and rolled around, foaming at the mouth. 9:21 Jesus asked his father, "How long has this been happening to him?" And he said, "From childhood. 9:22 It has often thrown him into fire or water to destroy him. But if you are able to do anything, have compassion on us and help us." 9:23 Then Jesus said to him, "'If you are able?' All things are possible for the one who believes." 9:24 Immediately the father of the boy cried out and said, "I believe; help my unbelief!"

9:25 Now when Jesus saw that a crowd was quickly gathering, he rebuked the unclean spirit, saying to it, "Mute and deaf spirit, I command you, come out of him and never enter him again." 9:26 It shrieked, threw him into terrible convulsions, and came out. The boy looked so much like a corpse that many said, "He is dead!" 9:27 But Jesus gently took his hand and raised him to his feet, and he stood up.

9:28 Then, after he went into the house, his disciples asked him privately, "Why couldn't we cast it out?" 9:29 He told them, "This kind can come out only by prayer."

Rabbi (9:5) Title of honor, often of a teacher

Day 17 Questions

Jesus tells us to pray and listen with all that we have. He also hears us when we need help in our unbelief.

1. Notice that Jesus pulls aside just three people to experience the transfiguration. Why do you think God does some things for big groups to see and other things for individuals to experience? (9:2-13)

2. Describe what you think Jesus looked like in the transfiguration. Why do you think his appearance was like this? (9:2-13)

3. Peter kept talking even though he didn't know what to say (9:6). Why do you think the voice from heaven said, "Listen to him"? (9:2-13)

4. The spirit in the boy was there "to destroy him" (9:22). Why do you think the father said, "I believe, help my unbelief"? Did he believe? (9:14-28)

Take a moment to reread this section.

1. What is one question you have from Day 17?

2. What is one phrase or idea that catches your attention or speaks to you from Day 17?

3. In a word or a short phrase, what is one thing you learned about Jesus from Day 17?

4. Based on what has happened in your life in the last 24 hours, why do you think God had you read this today?

Day 18 Reading

Second Prediction of Jesus' Death and Resurrection

9:30 They went out from there and passed through Galilee. But Jesus did not want anyone to know, 9:31 for he was teaching his disciples and telling them, "The Son of Man will be betrayed into the hands of men. They will kill him, and after three days he will rise." 9:32 But they did not understand this statement and were afraid to ask him.

Questions About the Greatest

9:33 Then they came to Capernaum. After Jesus was inside the house he asked them, "What were you discussing on the way?" 9:34 But they were silent, for on the way they had argued with one another about who was the greatest. 9:35 After he sat down, he called the twelve and said to them, "If anyone wants to be first, he must be last of all and servant of all." 9:36 He took a little child and had him stand among them. Taking him in his arms, he said to them, 9:37 "Whoever welcomes one of these little children in my name welcomes me, and whoever welcomes me does not welcome me but the one who sent me."

On Jesus' Side

9:38 John said to him, "Teacher, we saw someone casting out demons in your name, and we tried to stop him because he was not following us." 9:39 But Jesus said, "Do not stop him, because no one who does a miracle in my name will be able soon afterward to say anything bad about me. 9:40 For whoever is not against us is for us. 9:41 For I tell you the truth, whoever gives you a cup of water because you bear Christ's name will never lose his reward.
9:42 "If anyone causes one of these little ones who believe in me to sin, it would be better for him to have a huge millstone tied around his neck and to be thrown into the sea. 9:43 If your hand causes you to sin, cut it off! It is better for you to enter into life crippled than to have two hands and go into hell, to the unquenchable fire. 9:45 If your foot causes you to sin, cut it off! It is better to enter life lame than to have two feet and be thrown into hell. 9:47 If your eye causes you to sin, tear it out! It is better to enter into the kingdom of God with one eye than to have two eyes and be thrown into hell, 9:48 where their worm never dies and the fire is never quenched. 9:49 Everyone will be salted with fire. 9:50 Salt is good, but if it loses its saltiness, how can you make it salty again? Have salt in yourselves, and be at peace with each other."

Day 1 8 Questions

Jesus calls us to radically follow him, taking the form of a servant, just as Jesus himself did even to the point of death.

1. Why do you think the disciples, even though they were with him everyday, did not understand Jesus' teachings about his death and resurrection? (9:30-32)

2. How does it make you feel that even the disciples debated who was the "greatest"? What was Jesus' response? (9:33-37)

3. How should we look at other "groups" of true Christians who do great things but aren't in "our group"? (9:38-41)

4. Jesus uses an analogy about cutting off your hand, foot and eye. What point is he making? (9:42-49)

Take a moment to reread this section.

1. What is one question you have from Day 18?

2. What is one phrase or idea that catches your attention or speaks to you from Day 18?

3. In a word or a short phrase, what is one thing you learned about Jesus from Day 18?

4. Based on what has happened in your life in the last 24 hours, why do you think God had you read this today?

Day 19 Reading

Divorce

10:1 Then Jesus left that place and went to the region of Judea and beyond the Jordan River. Again crowds gathered to him, and again, as was his custom, he taught them. 10:2 Then some Pharisees came, and to test him they asked, "Is it lawful for a man to divorce his wife?" 10:3 He answered them, "What did Moses command you?" 10:4 They said, "Moses permitted a man *to write a certificate of dismissal and to divorce* her." 10:5 But Jesus said to them, "He wrote this commandment for you because of your hard hearts. 10:6 But from the beginning of creation *he made them male and female.* 10:7 *For this reason a man will leave his father and mother,* 10:8 *and the two will become one flesh.* So they are no longer two, but one flesh. 10:9 Therefore what God has joined together, let no one separate."

10:10 In the house once again, the disciples asked him about this. 10:11 So he told them, "Whoever divorces his wife and marries another commits adultery against her. 10:12 And if she divorces her husband and marries another, she commits adultery."

Jesus and Little Children

10:13 Now people were bringing little children to him for him to touch, but the disciples scolded those who brought them. 10:14 But when Jesus saw this, he was indignant and said to them, "Let the little children come to me and do not try to stop them, for the kingdom of God belongs to such as these. 10:15 I tell you the truth, whoever does not receive the kingdom of God like a child will never enter it." 10:16 After he took the children in his arms, he placed his hands on them and blessed them.

The Rich Man

10:17 Now as Jesus was starting out on his way, someone ran up to him, fell on his knees, and said, "Good teacher, what must I do to inherit eternal life?" 10:18 Jesus said to him, "Why do you call me good? No one is good except God alone. 10:19 You know the commandments: '*Do not murder, do not commit adultery, do not steal, do not give false testimony, do not defraud, honor your father and mother.*'" 10:20 The man said to him, "Teacher, I have wholeheartedly obeyed all these laws since my youth." 10:21 As Jesus looked at him, he felt love for him and said, "You lack one thing. Go, sell whatever you have and give the money to the poor, and you will have treasure in heaven. Then come, follow me." 10:22 But at this statement, the man looked sad and went away sorrowful, for he was very rich.

10:23 Then Jesus looked around and said to his disciples, "How hard it is for the rich to enter the kingdom of God!" 10:24 The disciples were astonished at these words. But again Jesus said to them, "Children, how hard it is to enter the kingdom of God! 10:25 It is easier for a camel to go through the eye of a needle than for a rich person to enter the kingdom of God." 10:26 They were even more astonished and said to one another, "Then who can be saved?" 10:27 Jesus looked at them and replied, "This is impossible for mere humans, but not for God; all things are possible for God."

10:28 Peter began to speak to him, "Look, we have left everything to follow you!" 10:29 Jesus said, "I tell you the truth, there is no one who has left home or brothers or sisters or mother or father or children or fields for my sake and for the sake of the gospel 10:30 who will not receive in this age a hundred times as much – homes, brothers, sisters, mothers, children, fields, all with persecutions – and in the age to come, eternal life. 10:31 But many who are first will be last, and the last first."

Day 19 Questions

Children are the quickest to believe in things that are "impossible." Jesus calls us to put our trust in Him even in the most difficult issues we face in life.

1. Why do you think Jesus teaches against divorce? How have you seen divorce affect your life or the life of your friends who have divorced parents? (10:1-12)

2. Jesus says that the only way to receive the kingdom of God, which is God's plan here on earth and for eternity, is to be like a child. What do you think it means to believe like a child? (10:13-16)

3. How would you answer the question the rich man asked Jesus, "What must I do to inherit eternal life?" (10:17)

4. What are some personal issues you face that seem "impossible" to solve? Why do you think Jesus says, "All things are possible with God"? Do you believe this? (10:18-31)

Take a moment to reread this section.

1. What is one question you have from Day 19?

2. What is one phrase or idea that catches your attention or speaks to you from Day 19?

3. In a word or a short phrase, what is one thing you learned about Jesus from Day 19?

4. Based on what has happened in your life in the last 24 hours, why do you think God had you read this today?

41

Day 20 Reading

Third Prediction of Jesus' Death and Resurrection

10:32 They were on the way, going up to Jerusalem. Jesus was going ahead of them, and they were amazed, but those who followed were afraid. He took the twelve aside again and began to tell them what was going to happen to him. 10:33 "Look, we are going up to Jerusalem, and the Son of Man will be handed over to the chief priests and experts in the law. They will condemn him to death and will turn him over to the Gentiles. 10:34 They will mock him, spit on him, flog him severely, and kill him. Yet after three days, he will rise again."

The Request of James and John

10:35 Then James and John, the sons of Zebedee, came to him and said, "Teacher, we want you to do for us whatever we ask." 10:36 He said to them, "What do you want me to do for you?" 10:37 They said to him, "Permit one of us to sit at your right hand and the other at your left in your glory." 10:38 But Jesus said to them, "You don't know what you are asking! Are you able to drink the cup I drink or be baptized with the baptism I experience?" 10:39 They said to him, "We are able." Then Jesus said to them, "You will drink the cup I drink, and you will be baptized with the baptism I experience, 10:40 but to sit at my right or at my left is not mine to give. It is for those for whom it has been prepared."

10:41 Now when the other ten heard this, they became angry with James and John. 10:42 Jesus called them and said to them, "You know that those who are recognized as rulers of the Gentiles lord it over them, and those in high positions use their authority over them. 10:43 But it is not this way among you. Instead whoever wants to be great among you must be your servant, 10:44 and whoever wants to be first among you must be the slave of all. 10:45 For even the Son of Man did not come to be served but to serve, and to give his life as a ransom for many."

Healing Blind Bartimaeus

10:46 They came to Jericho. As Jesus and his disciples and a large crowd were leaving Jericho, Bartimaeus the son of Timaeus, a blind beggar, was sitting by the road. 10:47 When he heard that it was Jesus the Nazarene, he began to shout, "Jesus, Son of David, have mercy on me!" 10:48 Many scolded him to get him to be quiet, but he shouted all the more, "Son of David, have mercy on me!" 10:49 Jesus stopped and said, "Call him." So they called the blind man and said to him, "Have courage! Get up! He is calling you." 10:50 He threw off his cloak, jumped up, and came to Jesus. 10:51 Then Jesus said to him, "What do you want me to do for you?" The blind man replied, "Rabbi, let me see again." 10:52 Jesus said to him, "Go, your faith has healed you." Immediately he regained his sight and followed him on the road.

Gentile (10:33) A non-Jewish person, people who do not support the Lord of the Old Testament

Day 20 Questions

Even as Jesus was approaching his death he was asking others what he could do for them along the way.

1. Jesus knew the exact details of his horrific torture and death in advance. What does this tell you about God's love? (10:32-34)

2. What is Jesus' advice to those who want to be "great"? How did Jesus live this out? (10:35-45)

3. The blind man was so desperate that he shouted at Jesus for help. Describe a time in your life that you needed the most help? (10:46-49)

4. Notice that Jesus asks the same exact question in verse 10:36 and 10:51. Based on their answers why do you think he granted one request but not the other? (10:50-52)

Take a moment to reread this section.

1. What is one question you have from Day 20?

2. What is one phrase or idea that catches your attention or speaks to you from Day 20?

3. In a word or a short phrase, what is one thing you learned about Jesus from Day 20?

4. Based on what has happened in your life in the last 24 hours, why do you think God had you read this today?

Day 21 Reading

The Triumphal Entry

11:1 Now as they approached Jerusalem, near Bethphage and Bethany, at the Mount of Olives, Jesus sent two of his disciples 11:2 and said to them, "Go to the village ahead of you. As soon as you enter it, you will find a colt tied there that has never been ridden. Untie it and bring it here. 11:3 If anyone says to you, 'Why are you doing this?' say, 'The Lord needs it and will send it back here soon.'" 11:4 So they went and found a colt tied at a door, outside in the street, and untied it. 11:5 Some people standing there said to them, "What are you doing, untying that colt?" 11:6 They replied as Jesus had told them, and the bystanders let them go. 11:7 Then they brought the colt to Jesus, threw their cloaks on it, and he sat on it. 11:8 Many spread their cloaks on the road and others spread branches they had cut in the fields. 11:9 Both those who went ahead and those who followed kept shouting, "_Hosanna! Blessed is the one who comes in the name of the Lord!_ 11:10 Blessed is the coming kingdom of our father David! Hosanna in the highest!" 11:11 Then Jesus entered Jerusalem and went to the temple. And after looking around at everything, he went out to Bethany with the twelve since it was already late.

Hosanna (11:9) A Greek form of a Hebrew word meaning, "O Save!", or "Save us!"
Temple (11:11) Formal meeting place in Jerusalem for all Jewish people, the center of their religion

Day 21 Questions

Jesus deserves a royal entrance from everyone. Even from those who eventually reject Him.

1. Jesus is on his way to Jerusalem where he will be killed. Though Jesus often avoided attention, why do you think he now takes this opportunity for a special entrance? (11:1-2)

2. The people shouted "Hosanna!" to Jesus as he passed by, which means "save us!" What would you shout if you were in that crowd? (11:3-9)

3. The same group of people who shouted "Hosanna" a few days later shouted "crucify him" [Mark 15:13]. How can a crowd influence, for better or worse, your feelings about Jesus? (11:9)

Take a moment to reread this section.

1. What is one question you have from Day 21?

2. What is one phrase or idea that catches your attention or speaks to you from Day 21?

3. In a word or a short phrase, what is one thing you learned about Jesus from Day 21?

4. Based on what has happened in your life in the last 24 hours, why do you think God had you read this today?

Day 22 Reading

Cursing of the Fig Tree

11:12 Now the next day, as they went out from Bethany, he was hungry. 11:13 After noticing in the distance a fig tree with leaves, he went to see if he could find any fruit on it. When he came to it he found nothing but leaves, for it was not the season for figs. 11:14 He said to it, "May no one ever eat fruit from you again." And his disciples heard it.

Cleansing the Temple

11:15 Then they came to Jerusalem. Jesus entered the temple area and began to drive out those who were selling and buying in the temple courts. He turned over the tables of the money changers and the chairs of those selling doves, 11:16 and he would not permit anyone to carry merchandise through the temple courts. 11:17 Then he began to teach them and said, "Is it not written: '*My house will be called a house of prayer for all nations*'? But you have turned it into *a den of robbers*!" 11:18 The chief priests and the experts in the law heard it and they considered how they could assassinate him, for they feared him, because the whole crowd was amazed by his teaching. 11:19 When evening came, Jesus and his disciples went out of the city.

The Withered Fig Tree

11:20 In the morning as they passed by, they saw the fig tree withered from the roots. 11:21 Peter remembered and said to him, "Rabbi, look! The fig tree you cursed has withered." 11:22 Jesus said to them, "Have faith in God. 11:23 I tell you the truth, if someone says to this mountain, 'Be lifted up and thrown into the sea,' and does not doubt in his heart but believes that what he says will happen, it will be done for him. 11:24 For this reason I tell you, whatever you pray and ask for, believe that you have received it, and it will be yours. 11:25 Whenever you stand praying, if you have anything against anyone, forgive him, so that your Father in heaven will also forgive you your sins."

The Authority of Jesus

11:27 They came again to Jerusalem. While Jesus was walking in the temple courts, the chief priests, the experts in the law, and the elders came up to him 11:28 and said, "By what authority are you doing these things? Or who gave you this authority to do these things?" 11:29 Jesus said to them, "I will ask you one question. Answer me and I will tell you by what authority I do these things: 11:30 John's baptism – was it from heaven or from people? Answer me." 11:31 They discussed with one another, saying, "If we say, 'From heaven,' he will say, 'Then why did you not believe him?' 11:32 But if we say, 'From people – '" (they feared the crowd, for they all considered John to be truly a prophet). 11:33 So they answered Jesus, "We don't know." Then Jesus said to them, "Neither will I tell you by what authority I am doing these things."

Day 22 Questions

Jesus' power is against greed and is unlimited for those with faith.

1. Why was Jesus angry with those who were selling and buying things in the temple courts? (11:15-19)

2. Though faith and God's actions are mysterious, what do verses 22 and 23 say about faith? (11:20-23)

3. Why do you think Jesus wants people not only to have faith but also forgiveness for others? (11:25)

4. Why do you think Jesus did not give a straight forward answer to those who wanted to assassinate him? [See 11:18] (11:27-11:33)

Take a moment to reread this section.

1. What is one question you have from Day 22?

2. What is one phrase or idea that catches your attention or speaks to you from Day 22?

3. In a word or a short phrase, what is one thing you learned about Jesus from Day 22?

4. Based on what has happened in your life in the last 24 hours, why do you think God had you read this today?

Day 23 Reading

The Parable of the Tenants

12:1 Then he began to speak to them in parables: "A man planted a vineyard. He put a fence around it, dug a pit for its winepress, and built a watchtower. Then he leased it to tenant farmers and went on a journey. 12:2 At harvest time he sent a slave to the tenants to collect from them his portion of the crop. 12:3 But those tenants seized his slave, beat him, and sent him away empty-handed. 12:4 So he sent another slave to them again. This one they struck on the head and treated outrageously. 12:5 He sent another, and that one they killed. This happened to many others, some of whom were beaten, others killed. 12:6 He had one left, his one dear son. Finally he sent him to them, saying, 'They will respect my son.' 12:7 But those tenants said to one another, 'This is the heir. Come, let's kill him and the inheritance will be ours!' 12:8 So they seized him, killed him, and threw his body out of the vineyard. 12:9 What then will the owner of the vineyard do? He will come and destroy those tenants and give the vineyard to others. 12:10 Have you not read this scripture:

'The stone the builders rejected has become the cornerstone.
12:11 This is from the Lord, and it is marvelous in our eyes'?"

12:12 Now they wanted to arrest him (but they feared the crowd), because they realized that he told this parable against them. So they left him and went away.

Paying Taxes to Caesar

12:13 Then they sent some of the Pharisees and Herodians to trap him with his own words. 12:14 When they came they said to him, "Teacher, we know that you are truthful and do not court anyone's favor, because you show no partiality but teach the way of God in accordance with the truth. Is it right to pay taxes to Caesar or not? Should we pay or shouldn't we?" 12:15 But he saw through their hypocrisy and said to them, "Why are you testing me? Bring me a denarius and let me look at it." 12:16 So they brought one, and he said to them, "Whose image is this, and whose inscription?" They replied, "Caesar's." 12:17 Then Jesus said to them, "Give to Caesar the things that are Caesar's, and to God the things that are God's." And they were utterly amazed at him.

Marriage and the Resurrection

12:18 Sadducees (who say there is no resurrection) also came to him and asked him, 12:19 "Teacher, Moses wrote for us: 'If a man's brother dies and leaves a wife but no children, that man must marry the widow and father children for his brother.' 12:20 There were seven brothers. The first one married, and when he died he had no children. 12:21 The second married her and died without any children, and likewise the third. 12:22 None of the seven had children. Finally, the woman died too. 12:23 In the resurrection, when they rise again, whose wife will she be? For all seven had married her." 12:24 Jesus said to them, "Aren't you deceived for this reason, because you don't know the scriptures or the power of God? 12:25 For when they rise from the dead, they neither marry nor are given in marriage, but are like angels in heaven. 12:26 Now as for the dead being raised, have you not read in the book of Moses, in the passage about the bush, how God said to him, 'I am the God of Abraham, the God of Isaac, and the God of Jacob'? 12:27 He is not the God of the dead but of the living. You are badly mistaken!"

—

Caesar (12:14) Roman emperor
Denarius (12:15) Roman silver coin representing a worker's daily wage
Sadducees (12:18) A small group of Jewish teachers who rejected many traditional teachings

48

Day 23 Questions

Jesus was misunderstood by nearly everyone he encountered. If you are following Jesus, you will encounter the same thing.

1. Based on the story Jesus tells about the vineyard, what will God do to those who reject his son Jesus? (12:1-12)

2. When the Pharisees and Herodians come to trap Jesus they give him false compliments ("you are truthful", "teach the way of God", "with the truth") How do you think Jesus was able to see "through their hypocrisy"? Is this applicable today? (12:13-17)

3. It is said that the Sadducees, who did not believe in the resurrection, were "sad-you-see" since they did not believe in a future after death. What do you think will happen after you die? Why? (12:18-27)

Take a moment to reread this section.

1. What is one question you have from Day 23?

2. What is one phrase or idea that catches your attention or speaks to you from Day 23?

3. In a word or a short phrase, what is one thing you learned about Jesus from Day 23?

4. Based on what has happened in your life in the last 24 hours, why do you think God had you read this today?

Day 24 Reading

The Greatest Commandment

12:28 Now one of the experts in the law came and heard them debating. When he saw that Jesus answered them well, he asked him, "Which commandment is the most important of all?" 12:29 Jesus answered, "The most important is: '*Listen, Israel, the Lord our God, the Lord is one.* 12:30 *Love the Lord your God with all your heart, with all your soul, with all your mind, and with all your strength.*' 12:31 The second is: '*Love your neighbor as yourself.*' There is no other commandment greater than these." 12:32 The expert in the law said to him, "That is true, Teacher; you are right to say that *he is one, and there is no one else besides him.* 12:33 And *to love him with all your heart, with all your mind, and with all your strength* and to love your neighbor as yourself is more important than all burnt offerings and sacrifices." 12:34 When Jesus saw that he had answered thoughtfully, he said to him, "You are not far from the kingdom of God." Then no one dared any longer to question him.

The Messiah: David's Son and Lord

12:35 While Jesus was teaching in the temple courts, he said, "How is it that the experts in the law say that the Christ is David's son? 12:36 David himself, by the Holy Spirit, said,
'The Lord said to my lord,
"Sit at my right hand,
until I put your enemies under your feet."'
12:37 If David himself calls him 'Lord,' how can he be his son?" And the large crowd was listening to him with delight.

Warnings About Experts in the Law

12:38 In his teaching Jesus also said, "Watch out for the experts in the law. They like walking around in long robes and elaborate greetings in the marketplaces, 12:39 and the best seats in the synagogues and the places of honor at banquets. 12:40 They devour widows' property, and as a show make long prayers. These men will receive a more severe punishment."

The Widow's Offering

12:41 Then he sat down opposite the offering box, and watched the crowd putting coins into it. Many rich people were throwing in large amounts. 12:42 And a poor widow came and put in two small copper coins, worth less than a penny. 12:43 He called his disciples and said to them, "I tell you the truth, this poor widow has put more into the offering box than all the others. 12:44 For they all gave out of their wealth. But she, out of her poverty, put in what she had to live on, everything she had."

David (12:35) A king, warrior, and poet from the Old Testament from around 1000 B.C.

Day 24 Questions

Jesus is not impressed if you look spiritually successful on the outside, but only if you are devoted on the inside.

1. Explain each aspect of Jesus' first answer regarding the most important commandment, "Love the Lord your God with all your" 1) Heart, 2) Soul, 3) Mind and 4) Strength (12:28-30)

2. What does it mean to "love your neighbor as yourself"? (12:31)

3. Jesus teaches us to "watch out" for those who are "experts" but are focused on their formal appearance, being greeted elaborately, and take the best seats for themselves. Why would he warn against people like this? (12:38-40)

4. How can the two coins worth less than a penny be "more" than the large amounts the rich people gave? (12:41-44)

Take a moment to reread this section.

1. What is one question you have from Day 24?

2. What is one phrase or idea that catches your attention or speaks to you from Day 24?

3. In a word or a short phrase, what is one thing you learned about Jesus from Day 24?

4. Based on what has happened in your life in the last 24 hours, why do you think God had you read this today?

Day 25 Reading

The Destruction of the Temple

13:1 Now as Jesus was going out of the temple courts, one of his disciples said to him, "Teacher, look at these tremendous stones and buildings!" 13:2 Jesus said to him, "Do you see these great buildings? Not one stone will be left on another. All will be torn down!"

Signs of the End of the Age

13:3 So while he was sitting on the Mount of Olives opposite the temple, Peter, James, John, and Andrew asked him privately, 13:4 "Tell us, when will these things happen? And what will be the sign that all these things are about to take place?" 13:5 Jesus began to say to them, "Watch out that no one misleads you. 13:6 Many will come in my name, saying, 'I am he,' and they will mislead many. 13:7 When you hear of wars and rumors of wars, do not be alarmed. These things must happen, but the end is still to come. 13:8 For nation will rise up in arms against nation, and kingdom against kingdom. There will be earthquakes in various places, and there will be famines. These are but the beginning of birth pains.

Persecution of Disciples

13:9 "You must watch out for yourselves. You will be handed over to councils and beaten in the synagogues. You will stand before governors and kings because of me, as a witness to them. 13:10 First the gospel must be preached to all nations. 13:11 When they arrest you and hand you over for trial, do not worry about what to speak. But say whatever is given you at that time, for it is not you speaking, but the Holy Spirit. 13:12 Brother will hand over brother to death, and a father his child. Children will rise against parents and have them put to death. 13:13 You will be hated by everyone because of my name. But the one who endures to the end will be saved.

The Abomination of Desolation

13:14 "But when you see *the abomination of desolation* standing where it should not be (let the reader understand), then those in Judea must flee to the mountains. 13:15 The one on the roof must not come down or go inside to take anything out of his house. 13:16 The one in the field must not turn back to get his cloak. 13:17 Woe to those who are pregnant and to those who are nursing their babies in those days! 13:18 Pray that it may not be in winter. 13:19 For in those days there will be suffering unlike anything that has happened from the beginning of the creation that God created until now, or ever will happen. 13:20 And if the Lord had not cut short those days, no one would be saved. But because of the elect, whom he chose, he has cut them short. 13:21 Then if anyone says to you, 'Look, here is the Christ!' or 'Look, there he is!' do not believe him. 13:22 For false messiahs and false prophets will appear and perform signs and wonders to deceive, if possible, the elect. 13:23 Be careful! I have told you everything ahead of time.

The Arrival of the Son of Man

13:24 "But in those days, after that suffering, *the sun will be darkened and the moon will not give its light;* 13:25 *the stars will be falling from heaven, and the powers in the heavens will be shaken.* 13:26 Then everyone will see *the Son of Man arriving in the clouds* with great power and glory. 13:27 Then he will send angels and they will gather his elect from the four winds, from the ends of the earth to the ends of heaven.

Day 25 Questions

Christians need to be aware of the challenges and deceptive people that appear as time runs out on earth as we know it.

1. Jesus knows the future. He knew that even the most beloved and famous place in their time, the temple, would not last forever. What does this mean for the famous places of our culture? (13:1-2)

2. Jesus makes it clear that Christians will face difficult challenges as time goes on. Why do you think Jesus tells this to people in advance? Would it be better if he did not tell them? How can we best prepare for the future? (13:9-13)

3. False and misleading people who would be able to do wondrous things were predicted by Jesus. Can people be misleading and deceptive even if they do "good" and "wonderful" things? Why? (13:14-27)

Take a moment to reread this section.

1. What is one question you have from Day 25?

2. What is one phrase or idea that catches your attention or speaks to you from Day 25?

3. In a word or a short phrase, what is one thing you learned about Jesus from Day 25?

4. Based on what has happened in your life in the last 24 hours, why do you think God had you read this today?

Day 26 Reading

The Parable of the Fig Tree

13:28 "Learn this parable from the fig tree: Whenever its branch becomes tender and puts out its leaves, you know that summer is near. 13:29 So also you, when you see these things happening, know that he is near, right at the door. 13:30 I tell you the truth, this generation will not pass away until all these things take place. 13:31 Heaven and earth will pass away, but my words will never pass away.

Be Ready!

13:32 "But as for that day or hour no one knows it – neither the angels in heaven, nor the Son – except the Father. 13:33 Watch out! Stay alert! For you do not know when the time will come. 13:34 It is like a man going on a journey. He left his house and put his slaves in charge, assigning to each his work, and commanded the doorkeeper to stay alert. 13:35 Stay alert, then, because you do not know when the owner of the house will return – whether during evening, at midnight, when the rooster crows, or at dawn – 13:36 or else he might find you asleep when he returns suddenly. 13:37 What I say to you I say to everyone: Stay alert!"

The Plot Against Jesus

14:1 Two days before the Passover and the Feast of Unleavened Bread, the chief priests and the experts in the law were trying to find a way to arrest Jesus by stealth and kill him. 14:2 For they said, "Not during the feast, so there won't be a riot among the people."

Jesus' Anointing

14:3 Now while Jesus was in Bethany at the house of Simon the leper, reclining at the table, a woman came with an alabaster jar of costly aromatic oil from pure nard. After breaking open the jar, she poured it on his head. 14:4 But some who were present indignantly said to one another, "Why this waste of expensive ointment? 14:5 It could have been sold for more than three hundred silver coins and the money given to the poor!" So they spoke angrily to her. 14:6 But Jesus said, "Leave her alone. Why are you bothering her? She has done a good service for me. 14:7 For you will always have the poor with you, and you can do good for them whenever you want. But you will not always have me! 14:8 She did what she could. She anointed my body beforehand for burial. 14:9 I tell you the truth, wherever the gospel is proclaimed in the whole world, what she has done will also be told in memory of her."

The Plan to Betray Jesus

14:10 Then Judas Iscariot, one of the twelve, went to the chief priests to betray Jesus into their hands. 14:11 When they heard this, they were delighted and promised to give him money. So Judas began looking for an opportunity to betray him.

Passover (14:1) Jewish festival celebrating their release from slavery in Egypt
Feast of Unleavened Bread (14:1) The day after Passover, really a continuation of Passover

Day 26 Questions

Jesus knew his days on earth were coming to an end. Our days are numbered too.

1. How is the fact that we have the Gospel of Mark, and even the Bible itself, a testament to Jesus' statement in verse 13:31? (13:28-31)

2. Why do you think Jesus says that "no one knows" the day or hour of the end of the world as we know it? What does this mean for the people who claim to know the exact date? (13:32-37)

3. Why do you think the woman came and poured the expensive oil on Jesus' feet? Was it a waste? (14:1-11)

Take a moment to reread this section.

1. What is one question you have from Day 26?

2. What is one phrase or idea that catches your attention or speaks to you from Day 26?

3. In a word or a short phrase, what is one thing you learned about Jesus from Day 26?

4. Based on what has happened in your life in the last 24 hours, why do you think God had you read this today?

Day 27 Reading

The Passover

14:12 Now on the first day of the feast of Unleavened Bread, when the Passover lamb is sacrificed, Jesus' disciples said to him, "Where do you want us to prepare for you to eat the Passover?" 14:13 He sent two of his disciples and told them, "Go into the city, and a man carrying a jar of water will meet you. Follow him. 14:14 Wherever he enters, tell the owner of the house, 'The Teacher says, "Where is my guest room where I may eat the Passover with my disciples?"' 14:15 He will show you a large room upstairs, furnished and ready. Make preparations for us there." 14:16 So the disciples left, went into the city, and found things just as he had told them, and they prepared the Passover.

14:17 Then, when it was evening, he came to the house with the twelve. 14:18 While they were at the table eating, Jesus said, "I tell you the truth, one of you eating with me will betray me." 14:19 They were distressed, and one by one said to him, "Surely not I?" 14:20 He said to them, "It is one of the twelve, one who dips his hand with me into the bowl. 14:21 For the Son of Man will go as it is written about him, but woe to that man by whom the Son of Man is betrayed! It would be better for him if he had never been born."

The Lord's Supper

14:22 While they were eating, he took bread, and after giving thanks he broke it, gave it to them, and said, "Take it. This is my body." 14:23 And after taking the cup and giving thanks, he gave it to them, and they all drank from it. 14:24 He said to them, "This is my blood, the blood of the covenant, that is poured out for many. 14:25 I tell you the truth, I will no longer drink of the fruit of the vine until that day when I drink it new in the kingdom of God." 14:26 After singing a hymn, they went out to the Mount of Olives.

The Prediction of Peter's Denial

14:27 Then Jesus said to them, "You will all fall away, for it is written,
'I will strike the shepherd, *and the sheep will be scattered.*'
14:28 But after I am raised, I will go ahead of you into Galilee." 14:29 Peter said to him, "Even if they all fall away, I will not!" 14:30 Jesus said to him, "I tell you the truth, today – this very night – before a rooster crows twice, you will deny me three times." 14:31 But Peter insisted emphatically, "Even if I must die with you, I will never deny you." And all of them said the same thing.

Gethsemane

14:32 Then they went to a place called Gethsemane, and Jesus said to his disciples, "Sit here while I pray." 14:33 He took Peter, James, and John with him, and became very troubled and distressed. 14:34 He said to them, "My soul is deeply grieved, even to the point of death. Remain here and stay alert." 14:35 Going a little farther, he threw himself to the ground and prayed that if it were possible the hour would pass from him. 14:36 He said, "Abba, Father, all things are possible for you. Take this cup away from me. Yet not what I will, but what you will." 14:37 Then he came and found them sleeping, and said to Peter, "Simon, are you sleeping? Couldn't you stay awake for one hour? 14:38 Stay awake and pray that you will not fall into temptation. The spirit is willing, but the flesh is weak." 14:39 He went away again and prayed the same thing. 14:40 When he came again he found them sleeping; they could not keep their eyes open. And they did not know what to tell him. 14:41 He came a third time and said to them, "Are you still sleeping and resting? Enough of that! The hour has come. Look, the Son of Man is betrayed into the hands of sinners. 14:42 Get up, let us go. Look! My betrayer is approaching!"

Day 27 Questions

Jesus was well aware that those around him would fail him in multiple ways, and yet He went ahead and followed God's plan obediently

1. The Passover was a time to remember that God passed over the sins of His people (Exodus 12:13). Why do you think Jesus chose this time of the year to go to Jerusalem and eventually to make his way to the cross? (14:12-16)

2. Jesus broke bread and the cup and shared it with his closest friends and disciples (This is called the Lord's Supper or communion today) even though he knew that they would "all fall away" in the coming hours. What does this say about Jesus' acceptance of us even though we are sinners? (14:13-31) Also see Romans 5:8.

3. Jesus prayed that God would change his plan when he prayed, "Take this cup from me." Why do you think Jesus prayed that? Why do you think Jesus' next words were, "Yet not what I will, but what you will"? (14:32-36)

4. People in Jesus' day often thought of the spirit as the soul and everything "inside" of a person was more or less the spiritual side of life. The flesh was considered the body and emotions of a person. When have you experienced a time that your spirit was willing, but your flesh was weak? (14:37-42)

Take a moment to reread this section.

1. What is one question you have from Day 27?

2. What is one phrase or idea that catches your attention or speaks to you from Day 27?

3. In a word or a short phrase, what is one thing you learned about Jesus from Day 27?

4. Based on what has happened in your life in the last 24 hours, why do you think God had you read this today?

Day 28 Reading

Betrayal and Arrest

14:43 Right away, while Jesus was still speaking, Judas, one of the twelve, arrived. With him came a crowd armed with swords and clubs, sent by the chief priests and experts in the law and elders. 14:44 (Now the betrayer had given them a sign, saying, "The one I kiss is the man. Arrest him and lead him away under guard.") 14:45 When Judas arrived, he went up to Jesus immediately and said, "Rabbi!" and kissed him. 14:46 Then they took hold of him and arrested him. 14:47 One of the bystanders drew his sword and struck the high priest's slave, cutting off his ear. 14:48 Jesus said to them, "Have you come with swords and clubs to arrest me like you would an outlaw? 14:49 Day after day I was with you, teaching in the temple courts, yet you did not arrest me. But this has happened so that the scriptures would be fulfilled." 14:50 Then all the disciples left him and fled. 14:51 A young man was following him, wearing only a linen cloth. They tried to arrest him, 14:52 but he ran off naked, leaving his linen cloth behind.

Condemned by the Sanhedrin

14:53 Then they led Jesus to the high priest, and all the chief priests and elders and experts in the law came together. 14:54 And Peter had followed him from a distance, up to the high priest's courtyard. He was sitting with the guards and warming himself by the fire. 14:55 The chief priests and the whole Sanhedrin were looking for evidence against Jesus so that they could put him to death, but they did not find anything. 14:56 Many gave false testimony against him, but their testimony did not agree. 14:57 Some stood up and gave this false testimony against him: 14:58 "We heard him say, 'I will destroy this temple made with hands and in three days build another not made with hands.'" 14:59 Yet even on this point their testimony did not agree. 14:60 Then the high priest stood up before them and asked Jesus, "Have you no answer? What is this that they are testifying against you?" 14:61 But he was silent and did not answer. Again the high priest questioned him, "Are you the Christ, the Son of the Blessed One?" 14:62 "I am," said Jesus, "and you will see *the Son of Man sitting at the right hand* of the Power and *coming with the clouds of heaven.*" 14:63 Then the high priest tore his clothes and said, "Why do we still need witnesses? 14:64 You have heard the blasphemy! What is your verdict?" They all condemned him as deserving death. 14:65 Then some began to spit on him, and to blindfold him, and to strike him with their fists, saying, "Prophesy!" The guards also took him and beat him.

Peter's Denials

14:66 Now while Peter was below in the courtyard, one of the high priest's slave girls came by. 14:67 When she saw Peter warming himself, she looked directly at him and said, "You also were with that Nazarene, Jesus." 14:68 But he denied it: "I don't even understand what you're talking about!" Then he went out to the gateway, and a rooster crowed. 14:69 When the slave girl saw him, she began again to say to the bystanders, "This man is one of them." 14:70 But he denied it again. A short time later the bystanders again said to Peter, "You must be one of them, because you are also a Galilean." 14:71 Then he began to curse, and he swore with an oath, "I do not know this man you are talking about!" 14:72 Immediately a rooster crowed a second time. Then Peter remembered what Jesus had said to him: "Before a rooster crows twice, you will deny me three times." And he broke down and wept.

Sanhedrin (14:55) The highest councils, or court, of Jews that met in Jerusalem

Day 28 Questions

Jesus knew his purpose and was willing to sacrifice it all,
even if others would not support him.

1. When Judas and the crowd came to arrest Jesus, all the disciples left and fled. How do you think this made Jesus feel? (14:43-51)

2. Jesus was guilty of no wrongdoing. Why do you think they wanted Him dead? (14:52-60)

3. Jesus gives his clearest verbal answer in the Gospel of Mark to his identity when He says, "I am" [the Christ, the Son of the Blessed One]. What do you think Jesus means by this? (14:61-65)

4. While Jesus was being questioned and beaten, Peter denies Jesus three times. When Peter realizes what he has done, he "broke down and wept." Why do you think he did this? Have you ever had a moment like this reflecting on your actions and Jesus' actions for you? (14:66-72)

Take a moment to reread this section.

1. What is one question you have from Day 28?

2. What is one phrase or idea that catches your attention or speaks to you from Day 28?

3. In a word or a short phrase, what is one thing you learned about Jesus from Day 28?

4. Based on what has happened in your life in the last 24 hours, why do you think God had you read this today?

Day 29 Reading

Jesus Brought Before Pilate

15:1 Early in the morning, after forming a plan, the chief priests with the elders and the experts in the law and the whole Sanhedrin tied Jesus up, led him away, and handed him over to Pilate. 15:2 So Pilate asked him, "Are you the king of the Jews?" He replied, "You say so." 15:3 Then the chief priests began to accuse him repeatedly. 15:4 So Pilate asked him again, "Have you nothing to say? See how many charges they are bringing against you!" 15:5 But Jesus made no further reply, so that Pilate was amazed.

Jesus and Barabbas

15:6 During the feast it was customary to release one prisoner to the people, whomever they requested. 15:7 A man named Barabbas was imprisoned with rebels who had committed murder during an insurrection. 15:8 Then the crowd came up and began to ask Pilate to release a prisoner for them, as was his custom. 15:9 So Pilate asked them, "Do you want me to release the king of the Jews for you?" 15:10 (For he knew that the chief priests had handed him over because of envy.) 15:11 But the chief priests stirred up the crowd to have him release Barabbas instead. 15:12 So Pilate spoke to them again, "Then what do you want me to do with the one you call king of the Jews?" 15:13 They shouted back, "Crucify him!" 15:14 Pilate asked them, "Why? What has he done wrong?" But they shouted more insistently, "Crucify him!" 15:15 Because he wanted to satisfy the crowd, Pilate released Barabbas for them. Then, after he had Jesus flogged, he handed him over to be crucified.

Jesus is Mocked

15:16 So the soldiers led him into the palace (that is, the governor's residence) and called together the whole cohort. 15:17 They put a purple cloak on him and after braiding a crown of thorns, they put it on him. 15:18 They began to salute him: "Hail, king of the Jews!" 15:19 Again and again they struck him on the head with a staff and spit on him. Then they knelt down and paid homage to him. 15:20 When they had finished mocking him, they stripped him of the purple cloak and put his own clothes back on him. Then they led him away to crucify him.

The Crucifixion

15:21 The soldiers forced a passerby to carry his cross, Simon of Cyrene, who was coming in from the country (he was the father of Alexander and Rufus). 15:22 They brought Jesus to a place called Golgotha (which is translated, "Place of the Skull"). 15:23 They offered him wine mixed with myrrh, but he did not take it. 15:24 Then they crucified him and divided his clothes, throwing dice for them, to decide what each would take. 15:25 It was nine o'clock in the morning when they crucified him. 15:26 The inscription of the charge against him read, "The king of the Jews." 15:27 And they crucified two outlaws with him, one on his right and one on his left. 15:29 Those who passed by defamed him, shaking their heads and saying, "Aha! You who can destroy the temple and rebuild it in three days, 15:30 save yourself and come down from the cross!" 15:31 In the same way even the chief priests – together with the experts in the law – were mocking him among themselves: "He saved others, but he cannot save himself! 15:32 Let the Christ, the king of Israel, come down from the cross now, that we may see and believe!" Those who were crucified with him also spoke abusively to him.

Day 29 Questions

Jesus endured a manipulated judge, flogging, mockery, abuse, crucifixion, and more: At any moment, he could have stopped it all. But, he did not.

1. Barabbas, a convicted criminal sentenced to death, was released instead of Jesus. The guilty man is freed (Barabbas) while the innocent man (Jesus) is condemned to death. Why do you think some Christians identify with Barabbas? Do you identify with Barabbas? How? (15:1-11)

2. Pilate handed over Jesus to be flogged (whipped) and crucified to "satisfy the crowd." (15:15) Pilate's decision was not based on facts, truth or compassion. How does our modern popular culture influence our own decision about Jesus? (15:12-15)

3. Note some of the terrible things that Jesus endured: flogging/whipping (15:15), crown of thorns (15:17), mocking (15:19), crucifixion (15:20), taking his last possessions (15:24), more verbal abuse and mockery (15:29-32). With Jesus as our example, what kind of things might today's Christian endure?

Take a moment to reread this section.

1. What is one question you have from Day 29?

2. What is one phrase or idea that catches your attention or speaks to you from Day 29?

3. In a word or a short phrase, what is one thing you learned about Jesus from Day 29?

4. Based on what has happened in your life in the last 24 hours, why do you think God had you read this today?

Day 30 Reading

Jesus' Death

15:33 Now when it was noon, darkness came over the whole land until three in the afternoon. 15:34 Around three o'clock Jesus cried out with a loud voice, "*Eloi, Eloi, lema sabachthani?*" which means, "*My God, my God, why have you forsaken me?*" 15:35 When some of the bystanders heard it they said, "Listen, he is calling for Elijah!" 15:36 Then someone ran, filled a sponge with sour wine, put it on a stick, and gave it to him to drink, saying, "Leave him alone! Let's see if Elijah will come to take him down!" 15:37 But Jesus cried out with a loud voice and breathed his last. 15:38 And the temple curtain was torn in two, from top to bottom. 15:39 Now when the centurion, who stood in front of him, saw how he died, he said, "Truly this man was God's Son!" 15:40 There were also women, watching from a distance. Among them were Mary Magdalene, and Mary the mother of James the younger and of Joses, and Salome. 15:41 When he was in Galilee, they had followed him and given him support. Many other women who had come up with him to Jerusalem were there too.

Jesus' Burial

15:42 Now when evening had already come, since it was the day of preparation (that is, the day before the Sabbath), 15:43 Joseph of Arimathea, a highly regarded member of the council, who was himself looking forward to the kingdom of God, went boldly to Pilate and asked for the body of Jesus. 15:44 Pilate was surprised that he was already dead. He called the centurion and asked him if he had been dead for some time. 15:45 When Pilate was informed by the centurion, he gave the body to Joseph. 15:46 After Joseph bought a linen cloth and took down the body, he wrapped it in the linen and placed it in a tomb cut out of the rock. Then he rolled a stone across the entrance of the tomb. 15:47 Mary Magdalene and Mary the mother of Joses saw where the body was placed.

The Resurrection

16:1 When the Sabbath was over, Mary Magdalene, Mary the mother of James, and Salome bought aromatic spices so that they might go and anoint him. 16:2 And very early on the first day of the week, at sunrise, they went to the tomb. 16:3 They had been asking each other, "Who will roll away the stone for us from the entrance to the tomb?" 16:4 But when they looked up, they saw that the stone, which was very large, had been rolled back. 16:5 Then as they went into the tomb, they saw a young man dressed in a white robe sitting on the right side; and they were alarmed. 16:6 But he said to them, "Do not be alarmed. You are looking for Jesus the Nazarene, who was crucified. He has been raised! He is not here. Look, there is the place where they laid him. 16:7 But go, tell his disciples, even Peter, that he is going ahead of you into Galilee. You will see him there, just as he told you." 16:8 Then they went out and ran from the tomb, for terror and bewilderment had seized them. And they said nothing to anyone, because they were afraid.

[Note: There is a longer ending to Mark that is not supported by the manuscript evidence. For more information see the introductory section of most Bibles.]

Day 30 Questions

Jesus died, but the grave could not contain him! Death comes to us all. Are you prepared for what is next?

1. Jesus cried out "my God, my God, why have you forsaken me". This can also be translated, "Why have you abandoned me?" In this important moment before Jesus' death, Jesus experienced the full impact of the consequences of sin, separation from a right relationship with God. What do you think that felt like for Jesus? (15:33-36)

2. When Jesus died, a curtain in the Temple, the symbolic place of God's presence that was reserved only for the highest order of priests, was torn from top to bottom. How can a tall curtain be torn from top to bottom? What does this signify about our access to God on our own? (15:37-41)

3. How would you feel if you were one of the disciples or one of the women who closely followed Jesus and saw him die, placed inside a tomb, and a stone rolled up to seal it? (15:42-47)

4. Jesus rose from the dead. What does this teach us about Jesus' identity? What can those who follow Jesus expect when they die? (16:1-8)

Take a moment to reread this section.

1. What is one question you have from Day 30?

2. What is one phrase or idea that catches your attention or speaks to you from Day 30?

3. In a word or a short phrase, what is one thing you learned about Jesus from Day 30?

4. Based on what has happened in your life in the last 24 hours, why do you think God had you read this today?

Notes

Made in the USA
Lexington, KY
04 June 2019